The Enneagram

A Comprehensive Guide to Understanding Personality Types and Unlocking the Secrets of the Enneagram to Discover Your True Self and Improve Relationships

Lewis Finan

Table of Contents

Introduction

Welcome to "The Enneagram: A Comprehensive Guide to Understanding Personality Types and Unlocking the Secrets of the Enneagram to Discover Your True Self and Improve Relationships."

In the journey of self-discovery and interpersonal connection, the Enneagram stands as a profound tool, guiding us through the labyrinth of human personality. Originating from ancient wisdom and refined through centuries of observation and study, the Enneagram offers a map—a map that illuminates the intricate pathways of our minds, emotions, and behaviors.

Within these pages, we embark on a voyage of exploration into the depths of the Enneagram, unraveling its mysteries and unlocking its transformative power. We will delve into the essence of the nine personality types, each offering a unique lens through which we perceive ourselves and the world around us. From the perfectionist drive of Type 1 to the free-spirited enthusiasm of Type 7, from the introspective depth of Type 4 to the grounded peace of Type 9, we will navigate the diverse landscapes of human nature.

But this journey is not just about understanding. It is about growth. It is about peeling back the layers of our personas to reveal the truth of who we are beneath. It is about recognizing our patterns, our fears, and our aspirations—and embracing them with compassion and courage. Through self-awareness and self-acceptance, we open the door to profound transformation and fulfillment.

Moreover, the Enneagram is not merely a solitary pursuit; it is a tool for building bridges between souls. As we come to understand ourselves more deeply, we also gain insight into the perspectives and motivations of others. We learn to communicate more effectively, empathize more authentically, and forge connections that transcend the barriers of personality.

Whether you are new to the Enneagram or a seasoned traveler on its pathways, this guide is designed to be a companion—a trusted companion that will accompany you on your quest for self-discovery and relational harmony. So, let us embark together, with open hearts and curious minds, as we journey into the transformative realm of the Enneagram.

Chapter 1: What is the Enneagram?

In the realm of understanding human personality and behavior, few systems rival the depth and insight offered by the Enneagram. Originating from ancient wisdom traditions, the Enneagram is a powerful tool that unveils the intricacies of the human psyche, shedding light on why we think, feel, and act the way we do.

At its core, the Enneagram is a symbol—a circle with nine interconnected points, each representing a distinct personality type. These nine types are not arbitrary categories but rather dynamic patterns that encompass a spectrum of traits, motivations, fears, and desires. Understanding the Enneagram begins with comprehending these fundamental types and the unique lens through which each perceives the world.

- **Type 1**: The Perfectionist, driven by a relentless pursuit of excellence and an inner critic that constantly demands improvement.
- **Type 2**: The Helper, defined by their altruism and a deep-seated need to be needed, often neglecting their own needs in favor of others.
- **Type 3**: The Achiever, ambitious and success-oriented, crafting a polished persona to garner admiration and validation.
- **Type 4**: The Individualist, marked by a quest for authenticity and a longing to express their unique identity, often grappling with feelings of inadequacy and longing.
- **Type 5**: The Investigator, intellectually curious and introverted, seeking knowledge and understanding as a means of navigating the world.

- **Type 6**: The Loyalist, vigilant and loyal, driven by a need for security and guidance, often oscillating between anxiety and loyalty.
- **Type 7**: The Enthusiast, adventurous and spontaneous, craving stimulation and avoiding pain through constant pursuit of new experiences.
- **Type 8**: The Challenger, assertive and self-reliant, fiercely protecting their autonomy and challenging authority.
- **Type 9**: The Peacemaker, easygoing and accommodating, seeking harmony and avoiding conflict by merging with others' agendas.

While each type possesses its strengths and virtues, they also harbor distinct pitfalls and blind spots, which the Enneagram illuminates with remarkable precision. Beyond merely labeling individuals, the Enneagram offers a roadmap for personal growth and transformation, inviting us to transcend our habitual patterns and embrace the full spectrum of human potential.

Central to the Enneagram's efficacy is its recognition of the interconnectedness of the nine types. Rather than existing in isolation, each type is influenced by its neighboring types, leading to a rich tapestry of relationships and dynamics. This dynamic interplay underscores the complexity of human nature, reminding us that our journeys are intrinsically linked to the collective human experience.

Moreover, the Enneagram acknowledges the fluidity and dynamism of personality, recognizing that individuals may exhibit traits from multiple types depending on context and development. This nuanced perspective fosters empathy and understanding, allowing us to appreciate the multifaceted nature of human identity without reducing it to simplistic categories.

Beyond its utility as a tool for self-awareness and personal growth, the Enneagram holds profound implications for our relationships, both personal and professional. By recognizing and honoring the diversity of personality types, we can cultivate deeper empathy and compassion for others, fostering healthier and more authentic connections.

In essence, the Enneagram is more than just a typology—it is a profound wisdom tradition that invites us to explore the depths of our psyche and humanity. As we embark on this journey of self-discovery and self-transformation, may we embrace the wisdom of the Enneagram with humility and reverence, knowing that it has the power to illuminate our path and enrich our lives in ways we never imagined possible.

1.1 Origins and History

The origins of the Enneagram trace back to ancient wisdom traditions, with its roots deeply embedded in various spiritual and philosophical teachings. While its precise origins remain shrouded in mystery, scholars suggest that the Enneagram may have originated in the mystical traditions of ancient Greece, Egypt, or the Middle East.

One of the earliest known references to the Enneagram can be found in the teachings of the Sufi mystic George Gurdjieff in the early 20th century. Gurdjieff, renowned for his esoteric insights and teachings on self-awareness and inner transformation, introduced the Enneagram as a tool for understanding the complexities of human personality and behavior.

However, it was not until the work of Chilean psychiatrist Oscar Ichazo in the 1960s that the Enneagram gained widespread recognition in the Western world. Drawing upon a diverse array of spiritual and psychological sources, including Sufism, Christianity, and Eastern mysticism, Ichazo developed a comprehensive system of nine personality types interconnected by a dynamic network of relationships.

Ichazo's teachings laid the foundation for further exploration and development of the Enneagram, particularly by Claudio Naranjo, a pioneering psychiatrist and psychotherapist. Naranjo expanded upon Ichazo's insights, integrating elements of modern psychology and psychotherapy to refine the Enneagram as a tool for self-awareness and personal growth.

In the following decades, interest in the Enneagram continued to grow, with numerous authors and teachers contributing to its dissemination and popularization. Today, the Enneagram enjoys widespread popularity across diverse fields, including psychology, business management, spirituality, and personal development.

While the Enneagram's ancient roots lend it a sense of timelessness and universality, its adaptation and evolution over the centuries reflect its relevance to the contemporary human experience. As we delve deeper into the origins and history of the Enneagram, we uncover a rich tapestry of wisdom that continues to inspire and empower individuals on their journey of self-discovery and self-transformation.

1.2 Core Concepts of the Enneagram

To truly grasp the essence of the Enneagram, one must delve into its core concepts, which serve as the foundational pillars of this profound wisdom tradition. At its heart, the Enneagram offers a comprehensive framework for understanding the intricacies of human personality and behavior, guiding individuals on a transformative journey of self-discovery and personal growth.

The Nine Personality Types:

Central to the Enneagram are the nine distinct personality types, each characterized by a unique set of traits, motivations, fears, and desires. These types serve as archetypal patterns that encompass the full spectrum of human experience, offering insight into why we think, feel, and act the way we do.

- **Type 1: The Perfectionist**: Driven by a relentless pursuit of excellence and a desire to uphold high standards, One is principled and conscientious, often striving for moral integrity and self-improvement.
- **Type 2: The Helper**: Defined by their altruism and compassion, Twos are nurturing and self-sacrificing, deriving fulfillment from meeting the needs of others while sometimes neglecting their own.
- **Type 3: The Achiever**: Ambitious and success-oriented, Threes are goal-oriented and image-conscious, seeking validation and admiration through their accomplishments and external recognition.
- **Type 4: The Individualist**: Marked by a deep sense of longing and introspection, Fours are creative and sensitive, driven by a desire for authenticity and a fear of being ordinary or mundane.
- **Type 5: The Investigator**: Intellectually curious and introspective, Fives are analytical and independent, seeking knowledge and understanding as a means of navigating the world while sometimes withdrawing into their inner world.
- **Type 6: The Loyalist**: Vigilant and loyal, Sixes are dutiful and security-oriented, often oscillating between anxiety and loyalty as they seek stability and guidance in an uncertain world.

- **Type 7: The Enthusiast**: Adventurous and spontaneous, Sevens are fun-loving and optimistic, constantly seeking new experiences and avoiding pain or discomfort.
- **Type 8: The Challenger**: Assertive and self-reliant, Eights are powerful and protective, fiercely defending their autonomy and challenging authority when necessary.
- **Type 9: The Peacemaker**: Easygoing and accommodating, Nines are harmonious and receptive, seeking inner and outer peace while sometimes avoiding conflict and assertiveness.

The Dynamics of Integration and Disintegration:

One of the most profound insights offered by the Enneagram is the dynamic nature of personality, which manifests through the processes of integration and disintegration. Each personality type is connected to two other types on the Enneagram symbol, forming a triangle of relationships.

Integration occurs when an individual adopts the positive traits of their connected type during times of growth and self-actualization. For example, a Type 5 may integrate towards Type 8, embodying qualities of assertiveness and decisiveness.

Conversely, disintegration occurs when an individual experiences stress or challenges, leading them to exhibit the negative traits of their connected type. Using the same example, a Type 5 may disintegrate towards Type 7, becoming scattered and distracted under stress.

Understanding these dynamics allows individuals to recognize their patterns of behavior and navigate the complexities of their inner world with greater clarity and insight.

The Wings:

In addition to their core personality type, individuals may also exhibit traits from one or both of the adjacent types on the Enneagram symbol, known as their "wings." These wings serve to enrich and nuance an individual's primary type, adding depth and complexity to their personality.

For example, a Type 4 with a 3 wing may display qualities of ambition and a desire for success, while a Type 4 with a 5 wing may exhibit more introverted and intellectual tendencies.

The Levels of Development:

The Enneagram recognizes that each personality type encompasses a spectrum of development, ranging from unhealthy to healthy expressions of behavior. At the lower levels of development, individuals may be dominated by their ego-driven patterns, leading to suffering and dysfunction.

However, through self-awareness and inner work, individuals can progress towards higher levels of development, embodying the virtues and qualities associated with their type in a more balanced and integrated manner.

The Triads:

The Enneagram further categorizes the nine types into three triads based on their primary emotional responses:

- **The Gut or Instinctive Triad (Types 8, 9, and 1)**: Characterized by a focus on instinctual reactions and gut feelings, individuals in this triad often struggle with issues of anger and control.
- **The Heart of Feeling Triad (Types 2, 3, and 4)**: Centered on themes of identity and validation, individuals in this triad grapple with issues of shame and worthiness.
- **The Head of Thinking Triad (Types 5, 6, and 7):** Driven by a need for understanding and security, individuals in this triad contend with issues of fear and anxiety.

By exploring these core concepts of the Enneagram, individuals can embark on a transformative journey of self-discovery and personal growth, unlocking the keys to greater self-awareness, compassion, and fulfillment in their lives.

1.3 The Nine Personality Types of the Enneagram

At the heart of the Enneagram lie the nine distinct personality types, each offering a unique lens through which individuals perceive and interact with the world. These types, rooted in deep-seated motivations, fears, and desires, shape our thoughts, emotions, and behaviors in profound ways. In this chapter, we will explore each of the nine personality types in detail, shedding light on their core characteristics, tendencies, and growth paths.

Type 1: The Perfectionist

Type 1 individuals are driven by a relentless pursuit of excellence and a profound sense of moral integrity. They possess a strong inner critic that constantly evaluates their actions against an ideal standard, leading to a perpetual quest for self-improvement and righteousness. While One strives for perfection in themselves and others, they can also be critical and judgmental, struggling to accept imperfection and ambiguity. However, when healthy, One channels their high standards into positive action, advocating for justice and integrity in all aspects of life.

Type 2: The Helper

Twos are characterized by their altruism and innate desire to support and nurture others. They derive fulfillment from meeting the needs of those around them, often sacrificing their well-being in the process. Twos excels in building deep, meaningful relationships and providing unconditional support and compassion to those in need. However, they may also struggle with boundary-setting and self-care, as they prioritize the needs of others above their own. Through self-awareness and healthy boundaries, Twos can cultivate a more balanced approach to giving and receiving love.

Type 3: The Achiever

Threes are driven by a relentless pursuit of success and achievement. They are highly goal-oriented and performance-driven, seeking recognition and validation for their accomplishments. Threes are skilled at presenting a polished image to the world, often excelling in leadership roles and competitive environments. However, they may struggle with authenticity and self-worth, as they equate their value with external achievements. By embracing vulnerability and cultivating a sense of intrinsic worth, Threes can find fulfillment beyond the pursuit of external validation.

Type 4: The Individualist

Fours are characterized by their depth of emotion and longing for authenticity. They possess a rich inner world and a keen sense of self-awareness, often grappling with feelings of uniqueness and existential longing. Fours are highly creative and introspective, expressing themselves through art, music, and literature. However, they may also struggle with self-doubt and melancholy, feeling misunderstood or different from others. Through embracing their inherent worth and connecting with others authentically, Fours can find beauty and meaning in their experiences.

Type 5: The Investigator

Fives are marked by their intellectual curiosity and need for understanding. They are analytical and insightful, seeking knowledge as a means of navigating the complexities of the world. Fives value independence and autonomy, often withdrawing into their inner world to recharge and reflect. However, they may struggle with social interactions and emotional expression, preferring solitude and introspection. By cultivating healthy relationships and sharing their insights with others, Fives can bridge the gap between intellect and emotion, finding fulfillment in both.

Type 6: The Loyalist

Sixes are characterized by their loyalty and vigilance. They are deeply attuned to potential threats and uncertainties, seeking security and guidance in an unpredictable world. Sixes are dependable and committed, forming strong bonds with family, friends, and community. However, they may also struggle with anxiety and doubt, second-guessing their decisions and seeking reassurance from others. Through building self-trust and embracing uncertainty, Sixes can cultivate courage and resilience in the face of adversity.

Type 7: The Enthusiast

Sevens are defined by their sense of adventure and optimism. They are spontaneous and fun-loving, constantly seeking new experiences and opportunities for excitement. Sevens excel at generating ideas and exploring possibilities, infusing joy and enthusiasm into every aspect of their lives. However, they may also struggle with impulsivity and avoidance, using distractions to escape from uncomfortable emotions or situations. By embracing mindfulness and staying present in the moment, Sevens can find fulfillment in the here and now.

Type 8: The Challenger

Eights are characterized by their strength and assertiveness. They are powerful and protective, fiercely defending their autonomy and standing up for what they believe in. Eights are natural leaders, unafraid to confront injustice or oppression wherever they encounter it. However, they may also struggle with vulnerability and control, fearing betrayal or weakness. By cultivating empathy and compassion for themselves and others, Eights can harness their strength for positive change and transformation.

Type 9: The Peacemaker

Nines are marked by their calm and easygoing nature. They seek harmony and unity, avoiding conflict and discord whenever possible. Nines are empathetic and accepting, valuing inclusivity and understanding in their relationships. However, they may also struggle with inertia and indecision, avoiding confrontation and prioritizing peace at any cost. By embracing their voice and asserting their needs, Nines can cultivate a sense of inner peace and authenticity in their lives.

In summary, the Enneagram offers a rich tapestry of personality types, each with its strengths, challenges, and growth opportunities. By exploring the intricacies of the nine types, individuals can gain deeper insights into themselves and others, fostering empathy, compassion, and personal growth along the way. Through self-awareness and intentional practice, we can embrace the full spectrum of human experience and unlock our true potential as individuals.

Chapter 2: Exploring the Nine Personality Types

In the previous chapter, we delved into the core concepts of the Enneagram and introduced the nine distinct personality types. Now, we embark on a deeper exploration of each type, uncovering their unique characteristics, motivations, and growth paths. By understanding the intricacies of the nine personality types, we gain valuable insights into ourselves and others, fostering empathy, compassion, and personal growth.

Type 1: The Perfectionist

Type 1 individuals are driven by a profound sense of moral integrity and a relentless pursuit of excellence. They possess a strong inner critic that constantly evaluates their actions against an ideal standard, leading to a perpetual quest for self-improvement and righteousness. Ones excel in roles that require attention to detail, precision, and adherence to rules and standards. However, they may struggle with perfectionism and self-criticism, finding it challenging to accept imperfections in themselves and others. By cultivating self-compassion and embracing flexibility, Ones can harness their high standards for positive change and growth.

Type 2: The Helper

Twos are characterized by their altruism and innate desire to support and nurture others. They derive fulfillment from meeting the needs of those around them, often sacrificing their well-being in the process. Twos excel in roles that involve caregiving, mentoring, and fostering meaningful connections with others. However, they may struggle with boundary-setting and self-care, as they prioritize the needs of others above their own. By practicing self-awareness and setting healthy boundaries, Twos can cultivate a more balanced approach to giving and receiving love.

Type 3: The Achiever

Threes are driven by a relentless pursuit of success and achievement. They are highly goal-oriented and performance-driven, seeking recognition and validation for their accomplishments. Threes thrive in environments that value ambition, leadership, and strategic thinking. However, they may struggle with authenticity and self-worth, as they equate their value with external achievements. By embracing vulnerability and cultivating a sense of intrinsic worth, Threes can find fulfillment beyond the pursuit of external validation.

Type 4: The Individualist

Fours are characterized by their depth of emotion and longing for authenticity. They possess a rich inner world and a keen sense of self-awareness, often grappling with feelings of uniqueness and existential longing. Fours excels in roles that allow for creative expression, introspection, and emotional depth. However, they may struggle with self-doubt and melancholy, feeling misunderstood or different from others. By embracing their inherent worth and connecting with others authentically, Fours can find beauty and meaning in their experiences.

Type 5: The Investigator

Fives are marked by their intellectual curiosity and need for understanding. They are analytical and insightful, seeking knowledge as a means of navigating the complexities of the world. Fives thrive in roles that allow for independent research, problem-solving, and intellectual exploration. However, they may struggle with social interactions and emotional expression, preferring solitude and introspection. By cultivating healthy relationships and sharing their insights with others, Fives can bridge the gap between intellect and emotion, finding fulfillment in both.

Type 6: The Loyalist

Sixes are characterized by their loyalty and vigilance. They are deeply attuned to potential threats and uncertainties, seeking security and guidance in an unpredictable world. Sixes excel in roles that require reliability, teamwork, and risk assessment. However, they may struggle with anxiety and doubt, second-guessing their decisions and seeking reassurance from others. By building self-trust and embracing uncertainty, Sixes can cultivate courage and resilience in the face of adversity.

Type 7: The Enthusiast

Sevens are defined by their sense of adventure and optimism. They are spontaneous and fun-loving, constantly seeking new experiences and opportunities for excitement. Sevens thrive in environments that foster creativity, innovation, and flexibility. However, they may struggle with impulsivity and avoidance, using distractions to escape from uncomfortable emotions or situations. By embracing mindfulness and staying present in the moment, Sevens can find fulfillment in the here and now.

Type 8: The Challenger

Eights are characterized by their strength and assertiveness. They are powerful and protective, fiercely defending their autonomy and standing up for what they believe in. Eights excel in roles that require leadership, assertiveness, and a willingness to confront injustice. However, they may struggle with vulnerability and control, fearing betrayal or weakness. By cultivating empathy and compassion for themselves and others, Eights can harness their strength for positive change and transformation.

Type 9: The Peacemaker

Nines are marked by their calm and easygoing nature. They seek harmony and unity, avoiding conflict and discord whenever possible. Nines excel in roles that promote cooperation, diplomacy, and inclusivity. However, they may struggle with inertia and indecision, avoiding confrontation and prioritizing peace at any cost. By embracing their voice and asserting their needs, Nines can cultivate a sense of inner peace and authenticity in their lives.

In this chapter, we have explored the intricate nuances of the nine personality types of the Enneagram. Each type offers a unique perspective on human nature, shedding light on the diverse ways in which individuals perceive and interact with the world. By understanding the core characteristics, motivations, and growth paths of each type, we gain valuable insights into ourselves and others, fostering empathy, compassion, and personal growth along the way. As we continue our journey of exploration and self-discovery, may we embrace the richness and complexity of the human experience, celebrating the diversity of personalities that make each of us unique.

Type 1: The Perfectionist

Type 1 individuals, often referred to as "Perfectionists," are characterized by their unwavering commitment to upholding high standards and moral principles. They possess an inner critic that constantly evaluates their actions and the world around them, striving for excellence in all endeavors. Rooted in a deep sense of duty and righteousness, One seeks to live up to their ideals and make the world a better place through their actions.

Core Characteristics:

- **High Standards**: One has a clear vision of how things should be and hold themselves and others to exacting standards. They excel in environments where rules and guidelines are clearly defined, and they have a clear sense of what is right and wrong.
- **Self-Discipline**: Driven by a strong sense of duty, Ones exhibit remarkable self-discipline and diligence in pursuing their goals. They are dependable and responsible individuals who can be relied upon to follow through on their commitments.

- **Inner Critic**: One has an internal voice that constantly critiques their behavior, pushing them to strive for perfection. While this inner critic can be a source of motivation, it can also lead to feelings of guilt and self-criticism when they fall short of their standards.
- **Idealism**: With a strong sense of right and wrong, One is deeply committed to making the world a better place. They are drawn to causes and organizations that align with their values and are willing to advocate for change to bring about a more just and equitable society.
- **Responsible**: One takes their responsibilities seriously and is conscientious in fulfilling their obligations. They are often seen as reliable and trustworthy individuals who can be counted on to do what is right, even in challenging circumstances.
- **Struggle with Anger**: Despite their composed exterior, One may struggle with repressed anger, particularly when one perceives injustice or hypocrisy. They may internalize their anger rather than express it outwardly, leading to feelings of resentment and frustration.

Growth Path:

While One possesses many admirable qualities, one may find oneself trapped in a cycle of perfectionism and self-criticism that hinders their personal growth. By embracing self-compassion and flexibility, One can learn to balance their high standards with a greater sense of acceptance and forgiveness.

- **Cultivate Self-Compassion**: Instead of harsh self-judgment, One can practice self-compassion and acknowledge that perfection is unattainable. By treating themselves with kindness and understanding, they can break free from the cycle of self-criticism and embrace their inherent worth.

- **Embrace Flexibility**: One can benefit from learning to adapt to unexpected circumstances and recognize that perfection does not always equate to happiness. By embracing spontaneity and allowing room for imperfection, they can experience greater joy and fulfillment in life.
- **Practice Mindfulness**: Mindfulness techniques can help one become more aware of their inner critic and learn to observe their thoughts without judgment. By cultivating mindfulness, they can develop greater emotional resilience and respond to challenges with greater equanimity.
- **Seek Balance**: Balancing high standards with a sense of flexibility and acceptance is key to One's personal growth. By striving for excellence while also recognizing their limitations, they can find a sense of peace and harmony within themselves.

In essence, Type 1 individuals bring a sense of integrity, responsibility, and dedication to everything they do. By embracing self-compassion and flexibility, they can harness their perfectionistic tendencies for positive change and personal growth, striving not for flawlessness, but for authenticity and inner peace.

Type 2: The Helper

Type 2 individuals, often referred to as "The Helpers," are characterized by their innate desire to support and nurture others. They possess a deep sense of empathy and compassion, finding fulfillment in meeting the needs of those around them. Rooted in a genuine concern for the well-being of others, Twos strives to create meaningful connections and provide unconditional support to those in their lives.

Core Characteristics:

- **Altruism**: Twos are selfless individuals who derive fulfillment from helping others. They are quick to offer assistance and support, often putting the needs of others before their own.
- **Empathy**: With a keen ability to understand and empathize with the emotions of others, Twos excels in roles that require compassion and interpersonal skills. They are skilled listeners who offer genuine understanding and support to those in need.
- **Generosity**: Twos are generous individuals who freely give their time, energy, and resources to help others. They find joy in acts of kindness and are often the first to offer help in times of need.
- **People-Oriented**: Twos thrive in social settings and enjoy building deep, meaningful relationships with others. They are adept at creating a sense of warmth and connection, making others feel valued and appreciated.
- **Need for Approval**: Despite their altruistic nature, Twos may struggle with a need for validation and approval from others. They may seek affirmation through acts of service and may feel unfulfilled if their efforts go unnoticed or unappreciated.
- **Boundary Challenges**: Twos may struggle with setting healthy boundaries and may overextend themselves in their efforts to help others. They may neglect their own needs and well-being in favor of taking care of others, leading to feelings of exhaustion and burnout.

Growth Path:

While Twos possess many admirable qualities, they may find themselves feeling depleted and unfulfilled if their own needs are consistently overlooked. By practicing self-care and setting healthy boundaries, Twos can learn to balance their desire to help others with their well-being.

- **Prioritize Self-Care**: Twos can benefit from prioritizing their own needs and well-being. By taking time to recharge and engage in activities that bring them joy and fulfillment, they can replenish their energy reserves and avoid burnout.
- **Set Boundaries**: Learning to set healthy boundaries is essential for Twos' personal growth. They can practice saying no to requests that exceed their capacity and communicate their own needs and limitations to others.
- **Develop Self-Awareness**: Twos can benefit from developing greater self-awareness and understanding of their motivations and desires. By exploring their own needs and desires, they can cultivate a greater sense of authenticity and fulfillment in their relationships.
- **Practice Assertiveness**: Twos can benefit from practicing assertiveness and advocating for their own needs and desires. By expressing their preferences and boundaries assertively, they can create more balanced and mutually satisfying relationships.

In essence, Type 2 individuals bring warmth, empathy, and generosity to their interactions with others. By practicing self-care and setting healthy boundaries, they can cultivate more fulfilling and authentic relationships while continuing to support and nurture those around them.

Type 3: The Achiever

Type 3 individuals, often referred to as "The Achievers," are characterized by their relentless drive for success and accomplishment. They possess a strong work ethic and a clear vision of their goals, striving to excel in every aspect of their lives. Rooted in a desire for recognition and validation, Threes are highly motivated and results-oriented individuals who excel in leadership roles and competitive environments.

Core Characteristics:

- **Ambition**: Threes are highly ambitious individuals who set ambitious goals and work tirelessly to achieve them. They are driven by a desire for success and recognition, often pursuing excellence in their careers, relationships, and personal endeavors.
- **Adaptability**: With a keen ability to read and respond to their environment, Threes are skilled at adapting to changing circumstances and seizing opportunities for advancement. They excel in roles that require flexibility, innovation, and strategic thinking.
- **Charisma**: Threes possess a natural charisma and charm that draws others to them. They are confident and outgoing individuals who excel in social settings and thrive in leadership roles.
- **Image-Consciousness**: Threes are highly attuned to their public image and strive to present themselves in the best possible light. They are skilled at cultivating a polished and professional persona that garners respect and admiration from others.
- **Competitiveness**: Driven by a desire to outperform others, Threes thrive in competitive environments where they can showcase their

talents and achievements. They are motivated by the prospect of success and are willing to work hard to attain it.

- **Fear of Failure**: Despite their outward confidence, Threes may struggle with a deep-seated fear of failure and inadequacy. They may feel pressured to maintain their image of success at all costs, leading to feelings of anxiety and stress.

Growth Path:

While Threes possess many admirable qualities, they may find themselves feeling unfulfilled if their pursuit of success is driven solely by external validation. By cultivating self-awareness and authenticity, Threes can learn to find fulfillment beyond the pursuit of external achievements.

- **Cultivate Authenticity**: Threes can benefit from cultivating a greater sense of authenticity and self-awareness. By exploring their values and desires, they can align their goals with their true passions and aspirations.
- **Embrace Vulnerability**: Threes can benefit from embracing vulnerability and acknowledging their fears and insecurities. By embracing their authentic selves, they can develop deeper connections with others and find greater fulfillment in their relationships.
- **Focus on Intrinsic Motivation**: Instead of seeking validation from external sources, Threes can focus on intrinsic motivation and find fulfillment in the process of pursuing their goals. By finding joy and satisfaction in their achievements, they can experience a greater sense of fulfillment and contentment.

- **Practice Mindfulness**: Mindfulness techniques can help Threes become more aware of their thoughts and emotions and cultivate a greater sense of inner peace and balance. By staying present in the moment, they can reduce stress and anxiety and find greater clarity and focus in their pursuits.

In essence, Type 3 individuals bring drive, ambition, and charisma to everything they do. By cultivating self-awareness and authenticity, they can find fulfillment beyond the pursuit of external validation and achieve a greater sense of balance and fulfillment in their lives.

Type 4: The Individualist

Type 4 individuals, often referred to as "The Individualists," are characterized by their depth of emotion and longing for authenticity. They possess a rich inner world and a keen sense of self-awareness, often feeling different or misunderstood by others. Rooted in a desire for self-expression and uniqueness, Fours are highly creative and introspective individuals who seek to find meaning and beauty in their experiences.

Core Characteristics:

- **Depth of Emotion**: Fours experience emotions deeply and intensely, often navigating a wide range of feelings and moods. They are highly attuned to their inner world and may struggle with feelings of melancholy or existential angst.

- **Creative Expression**: With a strong desire for self-expression, Fours excels in artistic pursuits such as writing, music, and visual arts. They use creativity as a means of exploring and expressing their innermost thoughts and emotions.
- **Longing for Authenticity**: Fours have a profound longing for authenticity and individuality, seeking to uncover their true selves amidst a world of conformity. They are drawn to experiences and relationships that allow them to express their unique identity and perspective.
- **Introspection**: Fours are introspective individuals who spend a significant amount of time reflecting on their thoughts, feelings, and experiences. They are introspective by nature, seeking to understand the deeper meaning behind their emotions and motivations.
- **Sense of Uniqueness**: Fours often feel different or misunderstood by others and may struggle with feelings of alienation or isolation. They value their sense of uniqueness and may resist conforming to societal expectations or norms.
- **Desire for Meaning**: Fours are driven by a desire to find meaning and significance in their lives. They are drawn to experiences and relationships that evoke a sense of depth and authenticity, seeking to uncover the deeper truths of existence.

Growth Path:

While Fours possess many admirable qualities, they may find themselves feeling stuck in a cycle of longing and melancholy that hinders their personal growth. By embracing self-acceptance and gratitude, Fours can learn to find beauty and meaning in their experiences, regardless of their circumstances.

- **Practice Self-Acceptance**: Fours can benefit from practicing self-acceptance and embracing all aspects of themselves, including their strengths and weaknesses. By cultivating self-love and compassion, they can learn to appreciate their unique identity and value.
- **Cultivate Gratitude**: Fours can benefit from cultivating a sense of gratitude for the beauty and richness of life. By focusing on the positive aspects of their experiences, they can shift their perspective from longing to appreciation and find greater fulfillment in the present moment.
- **Engage in Mindfulness**: Mindfulness techniques can help Fours become more present and grounded at the moment, reducing rumination and anxiety. By practicing mindfulness, they can cultivate a greater sense of peace and tranquility in their lives.
- **Seek Connection**: Fours can benefit from seeking connection with others who share their values and interests. By building supportive relationships and communities, they can feel validated and understood, reducing feelings of isolation and alienation.

In essence, Type 4 individuals bring depth, creativity, and authenticity to their interactions with others. By embracing self-acceptance and gratitude, they can learn to find beauty and meaning in their experiences, cultivating a greater sense of fulfillment and contentment in their lives.

Type 5: The Investigator

Type 5 individuals, often referred to as "The Investigators," are characterized by their intellectual curiosity and need for understanding. They possess a keen analytical mind and a thirst for knowledge, seeking to unravel the mysteries of the world around them. Rooted in a desire for competence and self-sufficiency, Fives are independent thinkers who value autonomy and intellectual autonomy.

Core Characteristics:

- **Intellectual Curiosity**: Fives possess a natural curiosity and thirst for knowledge, constantly seeking to expand their understanding of the world. They are avid learners who excel in environments that stimulate their intellect and challenge their assumptions.
- **Analytical Thinking**: With a keen analytical mind, Fives excels in problem-solving and critical thinking. They approach situations with logic and objectivity, seeking to uncover underlying patterns and connections.
- **Need for Privacy**: Fives value their independence and privacy and may retreat into solitude to recharge and reflect. They are comfortable spending time alone and may struggle with excessive social interaction or intrusion into their personal space.
- **Self-Sufficiency**: Fives value autonomy and self-sufficiency and may be reluctant to rely on others for support or assistance. They prefer to tackle challenges on their own and may feel uncomfortable asking for help or support.
- **Deep Focus**: Fives can deeply focus on their interests and pursuits, often immersing themselves in complex topics or projects for extended periods. They are driven by a desire to master their chosen fields and may become experts in their areas of expertise.
- **Detachment**: Fives may struggle with emotional expression and may appear reserved or detached in social situations. They prefer to approach life with a sense of detachment, avoiding emotional entanglements or excessive displays of sentimentality.

Growth Path:

While Fives possess many admirable qualities, they may find themselves feeling isolated or disconnected from others if they prioritize intellect over emotional connection. By cultivating empathy and vulnerability, Fives can learn to balance their intellectual pursuits with a greater sense of emotional intimacy and connection.

- **Cultivate Empathy**: Fives can benefit from cultivating empathy and compassion for others. By stepping into the shoes of others and considering their perspectives, they can develop a greater understanding of human emotions and experiences.
- **Practice Vulnerability**: Fives can benefit from practicing vulnerability and opening up to others about their thoughts and feelings. By sharing their inner world with trusted individuals, they can deepen their connections and foster a greater sense of intimacy and closeness.
- **Seek Connection**: Fives can benefit from seeking connection with others who share their intellectual interests and values. By building supportive relationships and communities, they can feel validated and understood, reducing feelings of isolation and alienation.
- **Balance Intellectual Pursuits**: Fives can benefit from balancing their intellectual pursuits with activities that nourish their emotional well-being. By engaging in hobbies or practices that promote relaxation and connection, they can cultivate a greater sense of balance and fulfillment in their lives.

In essence, Type 5 individuals bring intellectual curiosity, analytical thinking, and independence to their interactions with others. By embracing empathy and vulnerability, they can learn to foster deeper connections and find greater fulfillment in their relationships.

Type 6: The Loyalist

Type 6 individuals, often referred to as "The Loyalists," are characterized by their loyalty and vigilance. They possess a strong sense of duty and commitment to their beliefs and relationships, seeking security and guidance in an unpredictable world. Rooted in a desire for safety and stability, Sixes are dependable and trustworthy individuals who value loyalty and community.

Core Characteristics:

- **Loyalty**: Sixes are fiercely loyal individuals who prioritize their relationships and commitments. They are dedicated to supporting and protecting those they care about, often going to great lengths to ensure their well-being.
- **Vigilance**: With a keen awareness of potential threats and uncertainties, Sixes are vigilant and cautious in their approach to life. They are adept at anticipating problems and preparing for worst-case scenarios, seeking to mitigate risks and ensure their safety.
- **Need for Security**: Sixes values security and stability and may seek out structures and routines that provide a sense of predictability. They are drawn to institutions and systems that offer clear guidelines and expectations, providing a sense of safety in an uncertain world.

- **Questioning Mindset**: Sixes possess a questioning mindset and may be skeptical of authority and tradition. They are not afraid to challenge the status quo and may seek out alternative perspectives and viewpoints in their search for truth and understanding.
- **Community-Oriented**: Sixes value their connections and relationships with others and may seek out communities and groups that share their values and beliefs. They thrive in environments that foster a sense of belonging and camaraderie, finding strength in numbers.
- **Anxiety**: Despite their outward strength and resilience, Sixes may struggle with anxiety and fear, particularly in situations that feel uncertain or unpredictable. They may experience a constant sense of unease and may seek reassurance and validation from others.

Growth Path:

While Sixes possess many admirable qualities, they may find themselves feeling overwhelmed by fear and uncertainty if they prioritize security over growth. By cultivating courage and self-trust, Sixes can learn to navigate life's challenges with greater confidence and resilience.

- **Cultivate Courage**: Sixes can benefit from cultivating courage and facing their fears head-on. By stepping outside of their comfort zones and embracing new experiences, they can build confidence and resilience in the face of uncertainty.
- **Build Self-Trust**: Sixes can benefit from building self-trust and confidence in their abilities. By recognizing their strengths and capabilities, they can learn to trust themselves to navigate life's challenges with grace and resilience.

- **Challenge Negative Thoughts**: Sixes can benefit from challenging negative thoughts and beliefs that contribute to their anxiety and fear. By practicing mindfulness and cognitive-behavioral techniques, they can reframe negative thinking patterns and cultivate a more optimistic outlook on life.
- **Seek Support**: Sixes can benefit from seeking support from trusted friends, family members, or professionals. By opening up about their fears and insecurities, they can receive validation and encouragement, reducing feelings of isolation and anxiety.

In essence, Type 6 individuals bring loyalty, vigilance, and community-mindedness to their interactions with others. By cultivating courage and self-trust, they can learn to navigate life's uncertainties with greater confidence and resilience, finding strength in their connections and commitments.

Type 7: The Enthusiast

Type 7 individuals, often referred to as "The Enthusiasts," are characterized by their sense of adventure and optimism. They possess a boundless energy and an insatiable curiosity, constantly seeking new experiences and opportunities for excitement. Rooted in a desire for freedom and joy, Sevens are spontaneous and fun-loving individuals who embrace life with enthusiasm and zest.

Core Characteristics:

Sense of Adventure: Sevens have a natural sense of adventure and a thirst for exploration. They are always seeking new experiences and opportunities for excitement, eager to embrace life's endless possibilities.

- **Optimism**: With an innate sense of optimism, Sevens approach life with a positive outlook and an unwavering belief in their ability to overcome challenges. They see obstacles as opportunities for growth and are quick to find silver linings in even the most difficult situations.
- **Spontaneity**: Sevens are spontaneous and adaptable individuals who thrive in dynamic and ever-changing environments. They are quick to seize the moment and make the most of every opportunity that comes their way.
- **Joyfulness**: With a zest for life and contagious enthusiasm, Sevens bring joy and laughter wherever they go. They have a knack for finding humor in everyday situations and can lift the spirits of those around them with their infectious energy.
- **Avoidance of Pain**: Despite their outward optimism, Sevens may struggle with a fear of boredom or discomfort. They may avoid facing difficult emotions or situations, preferring to focus on the positive and avoid anything that might dampen their mood.
- **Restlessness**: Sevens may struggle with restlessness and a constant need for stimulation. They may find it challenging to sit still or commit to long-term projects, preferring to keep their options open and explore new opportunities as they arise.

Growth Path:

While Sevens possess many admirable qualities, they may find themselves feeling unfulfilled if they prioritize pleasure and excitement over deeper emotional connection. By embracing mindfulness and practicing self-discipline, Sevens can learn to find fulfillment beyond the pursuit of novelty and excitement.

- **Cultivate Mindfulness**: Sevens can benefit from cultivating mindfulness and learning to be present in the moment. By slowing down and savoring life's simple pleasures, they can find greater fulfillment and contentment in the here and now.
- **Practice Self-Discipline**: Sevens can benefit from practicing self-discipline and learning to delay gratification. By setting goals and committing to long-term projects, they can experience a deeper sense of accomplishment and satisfaction.
- **Embrace Emotional Depth**: Sevens can benefit from embracing their emotions and allowing themselves to experience the full range of human experiences. By facing difficult emotions head-on, they can develop greater emotional resilience and find deeper connections with others.
- **Seek Balance**: Sevens can benefit from seeking balance in their lives and finding harmony between excitement and stability. By recognizing when to indulge in adventure and when to prioritize rest, they can create a more fulfilling and sustainable lifestyle.

In essence, Type 7 individuals bring enthusiasm, optimism, and spontaneity to their interactions with others. By embracing mindfulness and practicing self-discipline, they can learn to find fulfillment beyond the pursuit of novelty and excitement, cultivating deeper connections and a greater sense of contentment in their lives.

Type 8: The Challenger

Type 8 individuals, often referred to as "The Challengers," are characterized by their strength and assertiveness. They possess a powerful presence and a willingness to confront injustice and protect the vulnerable. Rooted in a desire for autonomy and control, Eights are confident and decisive individuals who value integrity and authenticity.

Core Characteristics:

Strength: Eights are strong and resilient individuals who exude confidence and determination. They are natural leaders who are not afraid to take charge and make tough decisions, even in the face of adversity.

- **Assertiveness**: With a strong sense of self-assurance, Eights are assertive and direct in their communication. They are not afraid to speak their minds and stand up for what they believe in, often advocating for those who are unable to speak for themselves.
- **Protectiveness**: Eights have a strong sense of justice and a desire to protect the vulnerable. They are fiercely protective of their loved ones and will go to great lengths to ensure their safety and well-being.
- **Independence**: Eights value their autonomy and independence and may resist authority or control from others. They prefer to make

their own decisions and chart their life course, refusing to be held back by external limitations or constraints.

- **Vulnerability**: Despite their outward strength, Eights may struggle with vulnerability and fear of being perceived as weak. They may tend to conceal their emotions and project an image of invulnerability to the outside world.
- **Integrity**: Eights value integrity and authenticity and are not afraid to stand up for their principles, even in the face of opposition. They have a strong sense of right and wrong and are unwavering in their commitment to justice and fairness.

Growth Path:

While Eights possess many admirable qualities, they may find themselves feeling isolated or misunderstood if they prioritize control and dominance over vulnerability and connection. By embracing vulnerability and cultivating empathy, Eights can learn to harness their strength for positive change and transformation.

- **Cultivate Empathy**: Eights can benefit from cultivating empathy and compassion for others. By stepping into the shoes of others and considering their perspectives, they can develop a greater understanding of human emotions and experiences.
- **Embrace Vulnerability**: Eights can benefit from embracing vulnerability and acknowledging their fears and insecurities. By allowing themselves to be vulnerable, they can foster deeper connections with others and experience greater emotional intimacy.
- **Practice Humility**: Eights can benefit from practicing humility and recognizing that true strength lies in vulnerability and

openness. By acknowledging their limitations and seeking guidance from others, they can cultivate a greater sense of humility and openness to growth.
- **Channel Energy Constructively**: Eights can benefit from channeling their energy and assertiveness into constructive outlets, such as advocacy and leadership. By using their strength to champion causes they believe in, they can effect positive change in the world while staying true to their values.

In essence, Type 8 individuals bring strength, assertiveness, and integrity to their interactions with others. By embracing vulnerability and cultivating empathy, they can learn to harness their strength for positive change and foster deeper connections with those around them.

Type 9: The Peacemaker

Type 9 individuals, often referred to as "The Peacemakers," are characterized by their harmonious nature and desire for inner and outer peace. They possess a calm and easygoing demeanor, seeking to create harmony and unity in their relationships and environments. Rooted in a desire for tranquility and acceptance, Nines are empathetic and compassionate individuals who value cooperation and understanding.

Core Characteristics:

- **Harmony**: Nines have a natural inclination towards harmony and balance, seeking to create peace and unity in their interactions with others. They are diplomatic and tactful individuals who excel at resolving conflicts and mediating differences.

- **Easygoing**: With a relaxed and easygoing demeanor, Nines are adept at adapting to various situations and personalities. They are patient and tolerant individuals who prefer to avoid confrontation and conflict whenever possible.
- **Empathy**: Nines possess a deep sense of empathy and understanding towards others, often putting themselves in others' shoes to see things from their perspective. They are compassionate listeners who offer support and guidance without judgment.
- **Avoidance of Conflict**: Nines have a strong aversion to conflict and may go to great lengths to maintain peace and harmony in their relationships. They may suppress their own needs and desires to avoid rocking the boat or causing discord.
- **Desire for Unity**: Nines value unity and cooperation and may seek out environments and relationships that foster a sense of belonging and acceptance. They thrive in environments where everyone feels valued and respected for who they are.
- **Tendency towards Inertia**: Despite their desire for peace and harmony, Nines may struggle with procrastination and inertia. They may avoid making decisions or taking action, preferring to maintain the status quo rather than risk upsetting the balance.

Growth Path:

While Nines possess many admirable qualities, they may find themselves feeling stagnant or unfulfilled if they prioritize harmony over their own needs and desires. By embracing assertiveness and self-expression, Nines can learn to assert themselves and pursue their own goals and aspirations with confidence.

- **Practice Assertiveness**: Nines can benefit from practicing assertiveness and learning to express their needs and desires openly and honestly. By asserting themselves respectfully and assertively, they can build stronger relationships and create a greater sense of balance in their lives.
- **Set Boundaries**: Nines can benefit from setting healthy boundaries and learning to prioritize their own needs and well-being. By recognizing their limitations and asserting their boundaries with others, they can prevent feelings of resentment and maintain a greater sense of autonomy.
- **Engage in Self-Reflection**: Nines can benefit from engaging in regular self-reflection and introspection to gain clarity on their values and aspirations. By connecting with their inner selves, they can identify their passions and pursue activities that bring them joy and fulfillment.
- **Embrace Action**: Nines can benefit from embracing action and taking proactive steps toward their goals and aspirations. By breaking tasks down into manageable steps and taking consistent action, they can overcome inertia and achieve their dreams with confidence.

In essence, Type 9 individuals bring harmony, empathy, and understanding to their interactions with others. By embracing assertiveness and self-expression, they can learn to prioritize their own needs and desires while still fostering peace and unity in their relationships and environments.

Chapter 3: Understanding Enneagram Dynamics

The Enneagram is a powerful tool for understanding personality dynamics and interpersonal relationships. In this chapter, we will delve into the intricate dynamics of the Enneagram system, exploring how different types interact with one another and how these interactions shape our perceptions and behaviors.

1. The Enneagram as a System

At its core, the Enneagram is a dynamic system that maps out nine interconnected personality types, each with its distinct traits, motivations, and fears. These types are not static categories but rather dynamic patterns of behavior that evolve and interact with one another in complex ways.

2. The Nine Points of Connection

One of the key insights of the Enneagram is that each type is connected to two other types along lines of integration and disintegration. These lines represent the primary ways in which each type responds to stress and growth, influencing their behaviors and attitudes.

- **Integration Lines**: When individuals are in a state of growth or integration, they exhibit the positive traits associated with their integration points. For example, a Type 1 may integrate towards Type 7, embodying qualities of spontaneity and joyfulness.

- **Disintegration Lines**: Conversely, when individuals are under stress or in a state of disintegration, they exhibit the negative traits associated with their disintegration points. Continuing with the example of Type 1, they may exhibit traits of Type 4, such as pessimism and self-doubt.

Understanding these lines of connection can provide valuable insights into how each type responds to different situations and stressors, as well as how they can work towards personal growth and development.

3. Triads and Group Dynamics

In addition to individual connections, the Enneagram also highlights broader patterns of group dynamics through its triadic structure. The nine types are grouped into three triads based on their primary motivations and fears:

- **The Gut Triad (Types 8, 9, and 1)**: These types are primarily motivated by a need for autonomy and control. They may struggle with issues related to anger and assertiveness.
- **The Heart Triad (Types 2, 3, and 4)**: These types are driven by a need for love and validation. They may struggle with issues related to shame and self-worth.
- **The Head Triad (Types 5, 6, and 7)**: These types are motivated by a need for security and certainty. They may struggle with issues related to fear and anxiety.

Understanding these triadic dynamics can shed light on how different types interact within groups and how they can support one another in their personal growth journeys.

4. Conflict and Resolution

While the Enneagram provides valuable insights into personality dynamics and interpersonal relationships, it also recognizes that conflict is inevitable in human interactions. However, conflict can also be an opportunity for growth and transformation when approached with awareness and compassion.

By understanding the dynamics of the Enneagram and recognizing our patterns of behavior, we can navigate conflicts more effectively and work toward resolution and reconciliation. By embracing empathy and understanding, we can foster deeper connections and cultivate a greater sense of harmony and unity in our relationships.

In the following chapters, we will explore practical strategies for applying Enneagram insights to various aspects of life, including communication, leadership, and personal development. By integrating Enneagram wisdom into our daily lives, we can unlock our full potential and cultivate more meaningful and fulfilling relationships with ourselves and others.

3.1 Wings and Arrows

In the intricate web of the Enneagram, wings, and arrows add further depth to our understanding of personality dynamics. Wings refer to the adjacent personality types that influence and complement our core type, while arrows represent the lines of integration and disintegration that shape our responses to stress and growth.

Wings:

Each Enneagram type is believed to have two adjacent wings, which are the neighboring types that influence our personality traits and behaviors. While we primarily identify with our core type, we also exhibit certain characteristics of our wings, which add nuances to our personality.

For example, a Type 3, known as "The Achiever," may have a wing of Type 2, "The Helper," or Type 4, "The Individualist." The influence of these wings can manifest in different ways, shaping how the core type expresses its traits and motivations.

Understanding our wings can provide valuable insights into the complexities of our personalities, helping us recognize and embrace the diverse aspects of ourselves.

Arrows:

Arrows represent the lines of integration and disintegration that connect each Enneagram type to two other types. These lines indicate how individuals respond to stress and growth, either adopting positive traits from their integration points or exhibiting negative traits from their disintegration points.

For instance, a Type 9, "The Peacemaker," integrates with Type 3, "The Achiever," during periods of growth, embodying qualities of motivation and productivity. Conversely, they may disintegrate towards Type 6, "The Loyalist," under stress, displaying traits of anxiety and skepticism.

Understanding our arrows can illuminate how we navigate challenges and opportunities in life, guiding us towards paths of personal growth and transformation.

In the dynamic interplay of wings and arrows, we uncover the intricate tapestry of human personality, rich with complexity and potential. By exploring these facets of the Enneagram, we deepen our self-awareness and compassion, fostering greater understanding and harmony in our relationships and interactions.

3.2 Levels of Development

Within the Enneagram framework, each personality type can exhibit different levels of development, ranging from healthy to unhealthy. These levels reflect the degree to which individuals embody the core characteristics of their type and how these traits manifest in their thoughts, feelings, and behaviors.

Healthy Levels:

At healthy levels of development, individuals exhibit the positive traits associated with their Enneagram type in a balanced and integrated manner. They are self-aware, resilient, and capable of navigating life's challenges with grace and maturity. Healthy individuals can use their strengths to contribute positively to their relationships and communities, inspiring others with their wisdom and compassion.

Average Levels:

At the average levels of development, individuals display a mix of both positive and negative traits associated with their type. They may exhibit patterns of behavior that reflect their underlying motivations and fears, but these traits are not yet dominating their personality. Average individuals may struggle with occasional bouts of stress or insecurity but are generally able to function effectively in their daily lives.

Unhealthy Levels:

At unhealthy levels of development, individuals are consumed by the negative traits associated with their Enneagram type, leading to significant dysfunction and distress. They may exhibit extreme behaviors that are detrimental to themselves and others, such as manipulation, aggression, or withdrawal. Unhealthy individuals may feel trapped in patterns of self-destructive behavior and struggle to break free from their negative cycles.

Growth and Transformation:

Understanding the levels of development within the Enneagram can provide valuable insights into our patterns of behavior and the potential for growth and transformation. By recognizing how we may be operating at less-than-optimal levels, we can take steps to cultivate greater self-awareness and make positive changes in our lives.

Through self-reflection, mindfulness, and compassionate inquiry, we can move towards the healthy levels of development associated with our

Enneagram type. By embracing our strengths and confronting our limitations, we can unlock our full potential and live more fulfilling and authentic lives.

In the following chapters, we will explore practical strategies for moving towards greater levels of health and wholeness within the Enneagram framework, empowering us to become the best versions of ourselves and make meaningful contributions to the world around us.

3.3 Centers of Intelligence

Within the Enneagram system, the concept of centers of intelligence provides a framework for understanding how individuals process and respond to information. These centers represent three primary areas of human experience: the head center, the heart center, and the body center.

Head Center:

The head center, also known as the thinking center, is associated with cognitive processes such as analysis, planning, and decision-making. Individuals who primarily operate from this center tend to rely on logic and rationality to navigate the world. The types within the head center are:

- Type 5: The Investigator
- Type 6: The Loyalist
- Type 7: The Enthusiast

Heart Center:

The heart center, also known as the feeling center, is associated with emotional processes such as empathy, compassion, and interpersonal connection. Individuals who primarily operate from this center tend to be sensitive to the emotions of themselves and others, seeking meaningful relationships and connections. The types within the heart center are:

- Type 2: The Helper
- Type 3: The Achiever
- Type 4: The Individualist

Body Center:

The body center, also known as the instinctual center, is associated with physical sensations and instincts such as survival, safety, and gut feelings. Individuals who primarily operate from this center tend to be grounded and practical, relying on their instincts to guide their actions. The types within the body center are:

- Type 8: The Challenger
- Type 9: The Peacemaker
- Type 1: The Perfectionist

Understanding Centers of Intelligence:

Each center of intelligence offers valuable insights into how individuals perceive and engage with the world around them. By recognizing our dominant center and understanding its strengths and limitations, we can cultivate greater self-awareness and make more informed choices in our lives.

Moreover, the integration of all three centers is essential for holistic well-being and personal growth. By balancing our cognitive, emotional, and instinctual processes, we can achieve a greater sense of harmony and wholeness within ourselves.

In the following chapters, we will explore practical techniques for cultivating awareness and integration across the three centers of intelligence, empowering us to live more authentic, fulfilling lives aligned with our truest selves.

Chapter 4: Using the Enneagram for Personal Growth

In this chapter, we will explore how the Enneagram can be utilized as a powerful tool for personal growth and self-discovery. By delving deeper into our Enneagram type and understanding its dynamics, we can uncover insights that lead to greater self-awareness, resilience, and fulfillment in our lives.

1. Self-Reflection and Awareness

One of the primary benefits of the Enneagram is its ability to shine a light on our unconscious patterns of behavior and thought. Through self-reflection and awareness, we can begin to recognize how our Enneagram type influences our perceptions, motivations, and actions. By developing a deeper understanding of ourselves, we can make conscious choices that align with our values and aspirations, rather than reacting from a place of habit or fear.

2. Identifying Patterns and Triggers

Another valuable aspect of the Enneagram is its capacity to help us identify recurring patterns and triggers in our lives. By examining how our Enneagram type responds to stress, conflict, and uncertainty, we can uncover underlying fears and insecurities that may be holding us back. Armed with this awareness, we can develop strategies for managing our reactions and navigating challenging situations with greater ease and resilience.

3. Cultivating Empathy and Understanding

The Enneagram also fosters empathy and understanding towards ourselves and others. By recognizing that each Enneagram type has its unique perspective and motivations, we can cultivate compassion and empathy for the diverse experiences of those around us. This increased empathy can strengthen our relationships and deepen our connections with others, creating a more supportive and harmonious social environment.

4. Embracing Growth and Transformation

Ultimately, the Enneagram serves as a roadmap for growth and transformation, guiding us toward greater levels of self-awareness, authenticity, and wholeness. By embracing the insights gleaned from our Enneagram type, we can embark on a journey of personal development that leads to a more fulfilling and purposeful life. Through self-reflection, self-compassion, and a willingness to embrace change, we can unlock our full potential and create a future aligned with our deepest desires and aspirations.

In conclusion, the Enneagram offers a wealth of opportunities for personal growth and self-discovery. By harnessing its insights and tools, we can cultivate greater self-awareness, resilience, and compassion, leading to a more meaningful and fulfilling existence. In the following chapters, we will explore practical strategies for applying the Enneagram to various aspects of life, including relationships, career, and spiritual development, empowering us to live our best lives with authenticity and purpose.

4.1 Self-Discovery and Awareness

Self-discovery and awareness are essential components of personal growth and development. They involve delving into the depths of our psyche, exploring our thoughts, feelings, motivations, and behaviors to gain a deeper understanding of ourselves. The Enneagram, a powerful personality typing system, offers a unique framework for self-discovery and awareness, providing insights into our core personality traits, patterns, and tendencies.

Understanding the Enneagram:

The Enneagram is a dynamic system that categorizes individuals into nine distinct personality types, each with its own set of motivations, fears, and behaviors. These personality types are interconnected, forming a complex web of relationships and dynamics. Understanding the Enneagram begins with identifying our core type, the dominant personality pattern that shapes our worldview and influences our thoughts and actions.

Identifying Our Core Type:

Identifying our core Enneagram type is the first step in self-discovery through the Enneagram. This involves exploring the nine personality types and reflecting on which one resonates most deeply with our experiences and tendencies. Each Enneagram type has its unique characteristics and motivations, which are rooted in core fears and desires. By recognizing our primary type, we gain valuable insights into our personality structure and the driving forces behind our behavior.

Exploring Core Motivations:

Once we have identified our Enneagram type, we can delve into its core motivations, the fundamental desires and fears that underpin our thoughts and actions. For example, Type 1, known as "The Perfectionist," is motivated by a desire for integrity and excellence, driven by a fear of making mistakes or being corrupt. Understanding these core motivations allows us to gain clarity on why we behave the way we do and what drives our decision-making processes.

Recognizing Patterns and Triggers:

Self-discovery through the Enneagram also involves recognizing the recurring patterns and triggers that influence our behavior. These patterns may manifest in how we respond to stress, conflict, or uncertainty, and can shed light on underlying fears and insecurities. For example, a Type 6, known as "The Loyalist," may exhibit patterns of anxiety and skepticism when faced with uncertainty or change. By identifying these triggers, we can develop strategies for managing our reactions and breaking free from self-limiting patterns.

Cultivating Mindfulness and Presence:

Mindfulness and presence play a crucial role in self-discovery through the Enneagram. By cultivating a mindful awareness of our thoughts, feelings, and sensations in the present moment, we can observe our Enneagram type in action and gain insights into our inner workings. This heightened awareness allows us to respond to life's challenges with greater clarity and equanimity, rather than reacting impulsively or unconsciously. Practices such as meditation, mindfulness, and journaling can help cultivate this sense of presence and awareness.

Embracing Growth and Transformation:

Ultimately, self-discovery through the Enneagram is about embracing growth and transformation. By shining a light on our strengths, weaknesses, and blind spots, we can embark on a journey of personal development that leads to greater authenticity and wholeness. Through self-reflection, self-compassion, and a willingness to embrace change, we can unlock our full potential and create a life that reflects our deepest desires and aspirations.

Integrating Insights into Daily Life:

Self-discovery through the Enneagram is not just an intellectual exercise; it is a journey of self-exploration and transformation that extends into every aspect of our lives. By integrating the insights gained from the Enneagram into our daily practices and interactions, we can cultivate greater self-awareness, resilience, and authenticity. For example, recognizing our Enneagram type's tendencies can help us navigate challenging situations at work or in relationships with greater ease and clarity. Similarly, understanding our core motivations can guide us in making choices that align with our values and aspirations.

Seeking Support and Guidance:

Self-discovery through the Enneagram can be a deeply personal and introspective process, but it is also valuable to seek support and guidance from others along the way. Engaging in discussions with friends, family members, or Enneagram practitioners can provide fresh perspectives and insights into our personality dynamics. Additionally, participating in Enneagram workshops, retreats, or online communities can offer opportunities for deeper exploration and connection with others on a similar journey of self-discovery.

In conclusion, self-discovery and awareness through the Enneagram offer a pathway to deeper understanding and fulfillment. By exploring our Enneagram type, understanding our core motivations, and cultivating mindfulness and presence, we can embark on a journey of self-discovery that leads to greater self-awareness, resilience, and authenticity. Through self-reflection, self-compassion, and a willingness to embrace change, we can unlock our full potential and create a life that reflects our deepest desires and aspirations.

4.2 Overcoming Limiting Beliefs and Patterns

In our journey of personal growth and development, one of the most significant obstacles we face is the presence of limiting beliefs and patterns. These beliefs and patterns are deeply ingrained in our psyche and can hold us back from reaching our full potential. However, through self-awareness, mindfulness, and intentional action, we can overcome these obstacles and create a life filled with purpose, fulfillment, and authenticity.

Understanding Limiting Beliefs:

Limiting beliefs are negative or self-defeating thoughts that shape our perceptions of ourselves, others, and the world around us. These beliefs often stem from past experiences, childhood conditioning, or societal influences and can manifest as feelings of inadequacy, unworthiness, or fear of failure. Common limiting beliefs include:

- "I'm not good enough."
- "I don't deserve success."
- "I'm not worthy of love."

Recognizing Patterns of Behavior:

Limiting beliefs often manifest in patterns of behavior that reinforce our negative self-perceptions. These patterns may manifest as self-sabotage, procrastination, or avoidance of challenging situations. By recognizing these patterns, we can begin to understand the underlying beliefs that drive them and take steps to break free from their grip.

Challenging Our Beliefs:

The first step in overcoming limiting beliefs is to challenge their validity. This involves questioning the evidence supporting our beliefs and examining alternative perspectives. By challenging the validity of our beliefs, we can begin to weaken their hold on us and create space for new, more empowering beliefs to emerge.

Cultivating Self-Compassion:

Self-compassion is an essential component of overcoming limiting beliefs. It involves treating ourselves with kindness, understanding, and acceptance, especially in moments of struggle or self-doubt. By cultivating self-compassion, we can counteract the negative self-talk that often accompanies limiting beliefs and foster a greater sense of self-worth and resilience.

Practicing Mindfulness:

Mindfulness is another powerful tool for overcoming limiting beliefs. By practicing mindfulness, we can observe our thoughts and emotions without judgment, allowing us to recognize when limiting beliefs arise and choose how to respond to them. Mindfulness also helps us cultivate a greater sense of presence and awareness, enabling us to break free from automatic patterns of behavior and make conscious choices that align with our values and aspirations.

Replacing Limiting Beliefs with Empowering Beliefs:

Once we have identified and challenged our limiting beliefs, we can begin to replace them with more empowering beliefs that support our growth and well-being. This process involves intentionally cultivating positive affirmations and reframing negative self-talk into statements of self-empowerment and possibility. For example:

- "I am worthy of love and respect."
- "I have the power to create the life I desire."
- "I am capable of overcoming any challenge that comes my way."

Taking Action:

Overcoming limiting beliefs requires intentional action and a willingness to step outside of our comfort zones. This may involve setting goals, taking risks, and facing our fears head-on. By taking action despite our fears and doubts, we demonstrate to ourselves that we are capable of achieving our goals and living a life of purpose and fulfillment.

Seeking Support:

Finally, overcoming limiting beliefs is often a journey that is best undertaken with the support of others. Seeking support from friends, family members, or a trusted therapist can provide valuable insights, encouragement, and accountability along the way. Additionally, participating in support groups or workshops focused on personal growth and empowerment can offer opportunities for connection and shared learning.

In conclusion, overcoming limiting beliefs and patterns is a crucial step in our journey of personal growth and development. By recognizing and challenging our limiting beliefs, cultivating self-compassion and mindfulness, and taking intentional action toward our goals, we can break free from the constraints that hold us back and create a life filled with purpose, fulfillment, and authenticity. With determination, courage, and support from others, we can overcome our limiting beliefs and unlock our full potential to live a life of joy, abundance, and meaning.

4.3 Cultivating Compassion and Empathy

Compassion and empathy are essential qualities that foster connection, understanding, and support in our relationships with ourselves and others. Cultivating these qualities requires self-awareness, mindfulness, and a willingness to see the world through the eyes of others. In this chapter, we will explore strategies for cultivating compassion and empathy in our daily lives, fostering deeper connections, and creating a more compassionate world.

Understanding Compassion and Empathy:

Compassion is the ability to recognize and alleviate the suffering of others, while empathy is the capacity to understand and share the feelings of others. These qualities are essential for fostering meaningful connections, promoting social harmony, and building a more compassionate society. Cultivating compassion and empathy begins with cultivating a sense of self-awareness and empathy towards ourselves.

Practicing Self-Compassion:

Self-compassion is the foundation upon which compassion and empathy towards others are built. It involves treating ourselves with kindness, understanding, and acceptance, especially in moments of struggle or self-doubt. By practicing self-compassion, we can cultivate a greater sense of self-worth and resilience, enabling us to extend compassion and empathy to others more readily.

Developing Empathy:

Empathy is the ability to understand and share the feelings of others, putting ourselves in their shoes and seeing the world through their eyes. Developing empathy requires active listening, perspective-taking, and emotional attunement. By listening deeply to others and seeking to understand their experiences and emotions, we can cultivate empathy and foster deeper connections in our relationships.

Practicing Active Listening:

Active listening is a fundamental skill for cultivating empathy and compassion in our relationships. It involves fully engaging with others, paying attention to their words, emotions, and body language, and validating their experiences without judgment or interruption. By practicing active listening, we demonstrate our willingness to understand and support others, fostering trust and connection in our relationships.

Cultivating Perspective-Taking:

Perspective-taking is another important aspect of empathy, allowing us to see the world through the eyes of others and understand their experiences and emotions more deeply. This involves putting aside our preconceptions and biases and truly immersing ourselves in the perspectives of others. By cultivating perspective-taking, we can bridge the gap between ourselves and others, fostering greater understanding and empathy in our interactions.

Practicing Kindness and Generosity:

Acts of kindness and generosity are powerful ways to cultivate compassion and empathy in our daily lives. Simple gestures such as offering a listening ear, giving a compliment, or performing a random act of kindness can have a profound impact on others, creating feelings of connection, appreciation, and support. By practicing kindness and generosity, we can cultivate a culture of compassion and empathy in our communities and promote positive social change.

Cultivating Mindfulness:

Mindfulness is another key component of cultivating compassion and empathy. By cultivating a mindful awareness of our thoughts, feelings, and sensations in the present moment, we can become more attuned to the needs and experiences of others. Mindfulness also helps us cultivate a greater sense of presence and empathy, enabling us to respond to the suffering of others with compassion and understanding.

Engaging in Compassionate Action:

Finally, cultivating compassion and empathy involves taking action to alleviate the suffering of others and promote social justice and equality. This may involve volunteering, advocacy, or simply speaking up against injustice and oppression. By engaging in compassionate action, we can make a positive difference in the lives of others and contribute to building a more compassionate and empathetic society.

In conclusion, cultivating compassion and empathy is essential for fostering connection, understanding, and support in our relationships and communities. By practicing self-compassion, developing empathy, and engaging in acts of kindness and generosity, we can create a more compassionate and empathetic world where all individuals feel seen, heard, and valued. With mindfulness, self-awareness, and a commitment to taking compassionate action, we can cultivate a culture of empathy and compassion that transforms our relationships and promotes positive social change.

Chapter 5: Applying the Enneagram in Relationships

Relationships are a fundamental aspect of human experience, shaping our sense of belonging, connection, and fulfillment. However, navigating the complexities of relationships can be challenging, as individuals bring their unique personalities, communication styles, and emotional needs into the mix. In this chapter, we will explore how the Enneagram can be applied in relationships to deepen understanding, foster empathy, and promote harmony.

Understanding Relationship Dynamics through the Enneagram:

The Enneagram offers a valuable framework for understanding relationship dynamics by providing insights into the core motivations, fears, and behaviors of individuals. By identifying the Enneagram types of ourselves and our partners, we can gain deeper insight into our relational patterns and tendencies, as well as the underlying dynamics at play.

Recognizing Differences and Similarities:

One of the key insights of the Enneagram is that each type has its unique strengths, challenges, and perspectives. By recognizing and appreciating the differences between ourselves and our partners, we can foster greater understanding and acceptance in our relationships. At the same time, the Enneagram also highlights the commonalities and shared experiences that bind us together, fostering a sense of connection and empathy.

Communicating Effectively:

Effective communication is essential for healthy and thriving relationships. The Enneagram can provide valuable insights into our communication styles and preferences, as well as those of our partners. By understanding how each Enneagram type tends to communicate, we can adapt our communication approach to better meet the needs and preferences of our partners, fostering clearer, more open, and more compassionate communication.

Resolving Conflict:

Conflict is an inevitable part of any relationship, but it can also be an opportunity for growth and deeper connection when approached with awareness and empathy. The Enneagram offers insights into the underlying motivations and triggers that contribute to conflict in relationships. By understanding how our Enneagram types influence our responses to conflict, we can approach disagreements with greater compassion, empathy, and understanding, fostering resolution and reconciliation.

Supporting Each Other's Growth:

One of the greatest gifts we can offer our partners in a relationship is support for their personal growth and development. The Enneagram can serve as a powerful tool for supporting each other's growth by providing insights into our strengths, weaknesses, and areas for development. By understanding our partner's Enneagram type and the dynamics of their personality, we can offer encouragement, guidance, and compassion as they navigate their growth journey.

Deepening Intimacy and Connection:

Intimacy and connection are at the heart of fulfilling relationships, and the Enneagram can help deepen these aspects by fostering greater self-awareness, empathy, and understanding. By exploring our Enneagram types together and sharing our insights and experiences, we can cultivate a deeper sense of intimacy and connection in our relationships. The Enneagram also provides tools and practices for fostering emotional intimacy, such as active listening, vulnerability, and authentic communication.

Balancing Autonomy and Togetherness:

Balancing autonomy and togetherness is an ongoing challenge in relationships, as individuals seek to maintain their independence while also nurturing their connection with their partners. The Enneagram can guide finding this balance by highlighting the unique needs and preferences of each Enneagram type. By understanding our own and our partner's need for space, autonomy, and connection, we can create a relationship dynamic that honors and respects both individuality and togetherness.

In conclusion, the Enneagram offers a wealth of insights and tools for navigating relationships with greater awareness, empathy, and compassion. By applying the principles of the Enneagram in our relationships, we can deepen our understanding of ourselves and our partners, foster clearer and more compassionate communication, resolve conflicts with greater ease and understanding, support each other's growth and development, and deepen intimacy and connection. With mindfulness, self-awareness, and a commitment to nurturing our relationships, we can create fulfilling and harmonious partnerships that enrich our lives and support our personal growth and well-being.

5.1 Recognizing Interpersonal Dynamics

Interpersonal dynamics play a crucial role in shaping the quality and depth of our relationships. Understanding these dynamics is essential for fostering connection, communication, and mutual understanding between individuals. In this section, we will explore how the Enneagram can help recognize and navigate interpersonal dynamics effectively, leading to healthier and more fulfilling relationships.

The Influence of Enneagram Types:

The Enneagram provides valuable insights into the core motivations, fears, and behaviors of individuals based on their Enneagram types. Each Enneagram type has its own unique perspective, communication style, and approach to relationships, which can influence how individuals interact with one another. By recognizing the Enneagram types of ourselves and others, we can gain deeper insight into the interpersonal dynamics at play and navigate them with greater awareness and empathy.

Identifying Communication Styles:

Communication styles vary widely among individuals and are influenced by factors such as personality, upbringing, and life experiences. The Enneagram offers insights into how each Enneagram type tends to communicate, allowing us to recognize and adapt to different communication styles more effectively. For example, Type 1s may communicate with clarity and precision, while Type 2s may express themselves with warmth and empathy. By understanding these differences, we can communicate more effectively and avoid misunderstandings in our relationships.

Understanding Conflict Resolution Styles:

Conflict is a natural part of any relationship, but how individuals approach and resolve conflict can vary significantly based on their Enneagram types. Some individuals may prefer to address conflict head-on, while others may avoid confrontation altogether. The Enneagram can help us understand our own and others' conflict resolution styles, enabling us to navigate conflicts with greater sensitivity and understanding. By recognizing and respecting each other's approaches to conflict resolution, we can resolve disagreements more effectively and strengthen our relationships in the process.

Exploring Attachment Styles:

Attachment styles play a significant role in shaping how individuals form and maintain relationships. The Enneagram can provide insights into our attachment styles based on our Enneagram types, shedding light on how we relate to others emotionally and behaviorally. For example, Type 6s may have a more anxious or fearful attachment style, while Type 9s may exhibit a more relaxed or avoidant attachment style. By understanding our attachment styles, we can cultivate healthier and more secure relationships grounded in trust and mutual respect.

Recognizing Defense Mechanisms:

Defense mechanisms are unconscious psychological strategies that individuals use to protect themselves from emotional pain or discomfort. These mechanisms can manifest in various ways, such as denial, projection, or rationalization. The Enneagram can help us recognize our own and others' defense mechanisms based on our Enneagram types, enabling us to navigate challenging situations with greater awareness and compassion. By understanding the underlying fears and insecurities that drive these defense mechanisms, we can respond to them with empathy and understanding, fostering deeper connection and trust in our relationships.

Navigating Power Dynamics:

Power dynamics often emerge in relationships as individuals navigate issues of control, influence, and authority. The Enneagram can shed light on how power dynamics play out based on individuals' Enneagram types and core motivations. For example, Type 8s may assert their dominance and authority in relationships, while Type 2s may seek validation and approval from others. By recognizing and understanding these dynamics, we can navigate power struggles more effectively and create relationships based on mutual respect and equality.

Fostering Emotional Intimacy:

Emotional intimacy is the foundation of deep and meaningful relationships, but it requires vulnerability, trust, and open communication. The Enneagram can help us foster emotional intimacy by providing insights into our emotional needs, fears, and vulnerabilities based on our Enneagram types. By sharing our Enneagram insights with our partners and creating a safe space for open and honest communication, we can deepen our emotional connection and strengthen our bond in our relationships.

In conclusion, recognizing interpersonal dynamics through the Enneagram is essential for fostering healthier, more fulfilling relationships. By understanding how Enneagram types influence communication styles, conflict resolution approaches, attachment styles, defense mechanisms, power dynamics, and emotional intimacy, we can navigate relationships with greater awareness, empathy, and compassion. With mindfulness, self-awareness, and a commitment to nurturing our relationships, we can create deep and meaningful connections that enrich our lives and support our personal growth and well-being.

5.2 Communication Strategies for Each Enneagram Type

Effective communication is the cornerstone of healthy and fulfilling relationships. However, each Enneagram type has its unique communication style, preferences, and challenges. In this section, we will explore communication strategies tailored to each Enneagram type, enabling individuals to communicate more effectively and foster deeper connections in their relationships.

Type 1: The Perfectionist

Type 1s are principled and conscientious individuals who value integrity and excellence. When communicating with a Type 1, it's essential to be clear, concise, and factual. Avoid exaggeration or hyperbole, as Type 1s appreciate honesty and accuracy. Provide constructive feedback in a respectful and non-judgmental manner, focusing on solutions rather than criticism. Acknowledge their efforts and attention to detail, reinforcing their sense of competence and dedication.

Type 2: The Helper

Type 2s are empathetic and nurturing individuals who prioritize the needs of others. When communicating with a Type 2, express appreciation for their kindness and generosity. Be attentive and empathetic, acknowledging their emotions and concerns. Encourage them to express their own needs and boundaries, as Type 2s often prioritize the needs of others over their own. Offer validation and support, affirming their worthiness and value as individuals.

Type 3: The Achiever

Type 3s are ambitious and driven individuals who value success and recognition. When communicating with a Type 3, focus on goals, achievements, and tangible results. Provide clear expectations and feedback, highlighting their strengths and accomplishments. Acknowledge their hard work and dedication, reinforcing their sense of competence and accomplishment. Encourage them to express their authentic thoughts and feelings, beyond their external achievements.

Type 4: The Individualist

Type 4s are introspective and creative individuals who value authenticity and self-expression. When communicating with a Type 4, acknowledge their unique perspective and creativity. Listen actively and empathetically, validating their emotions and experiences. Avoid dismissing or minimizing their feelings, as Type 4s crave validation and understanding. Encourage them to express themselves authentically, allowing space for their emotional depth and complexity.

Type 5: The Investigator

Type 5s are analytical and independent individuals who value knowledge and expertise. When communicating with a Type 5, respect their need for privacy and autonomy. Provide clear and logical explanations, avoiding emotional appeals or pressure tactics. Allow them space to process information independently and encourage them to share their insights and expertise. Acknowledge their intelligence and resourcefulness, fostering a sense of respect and trust in the relationship.

Type 6: The Loyalist

Type 6s are loyal and cautious individuals who value security and stability. When communicating with a Type 6, provide reassurance and support, acknowledging their concerns and anxieties. Be patient and understanding, as Type 6s may seek validation and reassurance in uncertain situations. Encourage open and honest communication, fostering trust and transparency in the relationship. Offer practical solutions and guidance, helping them navigate their fears and uncertainties.

Type 7: The Enthusiast

Type 7s are spontaneous and optimistic individuals who value freedom and adventure. When communicating with a Type 7, be upbeat, focusing on opportunities and possibilities. Encourage them to explore new ideas and experiences, allowing space for their enthusiasm and creativity. Avoid dwelling on pessimistic topics, as Type 7s may prefer to focus on the present moment and future possibilities. Provide structure and support when needed, helping them follow through on their goals and commitments.

Type 8: The Challenger

Type 8s are assertive and confident individuals who value strength and autonomy. When communicating with a Type 8, be direct and assertive, avoiding passive-aggressive or manipulative behavior. Respect their boundaries and autonomy, acknowledging their need for independence and control. Encourage open and honest communication, allowing space for their opinions and perspectives. Be willing to stand up for yourself and assert your boundaries, as Type 8s respect individuals who are confident and self-assured.

Type 9: The Peacemaker

Type 9s are easygoing and empathetic individuals who value harmony and peace. When communicating with a Type 9, be patient and understanding, acknowledging their desire for harmony and consensus. Avoid confrontation or conflict, as Type 9s may prefer to avoid conflict and maintain peace at all costs. Encourage them to express their own opinions and preferences, as Type 9s may tend to defer to others' desires. Foster a supportive and inclusive environment, where all voices are heard and respected.

In conclusion, effective communication is essential for fostering healthy and fulfilling relationships. By understanding the communication styles and preferences of each Enneagram type, individuals can tailor their communication strategies to better connect with others and promote understanding, empathy, and mutual respect in their relationships. With mindfulness, empathy, and a commitment to clear and authentic communication, individuals can create deeper and more meaningful connections with their partners, friends, and colleagues.

5.3 Resolving Conflict and Strengthening Bonds

Conflict is a natural and inevitable part of any relationship. However, how we navigate and resolve conflict can significantly impact the health and longevity of our relationships. In this section, we will explore strategies for resolving conflict and strengthening bonds using insights from the Enneagram, fostering deeper understanding, empathy, and connection in our relationships.

Understanding the Root of Conflict:

Conflict often arises from differences in values, perspectives, or needs between individuals. These differences can trigger emotional reactions and defensive behaviors, leading to tension and discord in the relationship. By understanding the underlying motivations and fears of each Enneagram type, we can gain insight into the root causes of conflict and approach resolution with greater empathy and understanding.

Practicing Active Listening:

Active listening is a foundational skill for resolving conflict and strengthening bonds in relationships. It involves fully engaging with the other person, and paying attention to their words, emotions, and body language without judgment or interruption. By listening actively and empathetically, we can validate the other person's perspective and create a safe space for open and honest communication, fostering understanding and connection.

Validating Emotions and Perspectives:

Validation is essential for resolving conflict and building trust in relationships. It involves acknowledging and accepting the other person's emotions and perspectives, even if we may disagree with them. By validating the other person's experiences and feelings, we demonstrate empathy and respect, laying the groundwork for productive dialogue and resolution.

Expressing Needs and Boundaries:

Effective conflict resolution requires individuals to express their own needs and boundaries clearly and assertively. By communicating our needs and boundaries in a respectful and non-confrontational manner, we create space for mutual understanding and compromise. It's essential to assert our boundaries while also remaining open to the other person's perspective, fostering a sense of respect and collaboration in the resolution process.

Finding Common Ground:

Finding common ground is key to resolving conflict and strengthening bonds in relationships. By identifying shared goals, values, or interests, individuals can bridge the gap between their differences and work together towards a mutually beneficial solution. Finding common ground also fosters a sense of connection and solidarity, reinforcing the bonds of the relationship.

Collaborative Problem-Solving:

Collaborative problem-solving is a constructive approach to conflict resolution that involves working together to find creative solutions to the underlying issues. By brainstorming ideas, exploring different perspectives, and considering the needs of all parties involved, individuals can identify solutions that address the root causes of conflict and promote mutual satisfaction and understanding.

Cultivating Empathy and Understanding:

Empathy is a powerful tool for resolving conflict and strengthening bonds in relationships. By putting ourselves in the other person's shoes and seeing the situation from their perspective, we can gain insight into their feelings, motivations, and needs. Cultivating empathy fosters a sense of connection and compassion, enabling individuals to navigate conflict with greater sensitivity and understanding.

Practicing Forgiveness and Letting Go:

Forgiveness is essential for healing wounds and moving forward in relationships. By letting go of resentment and grudges, individuals can release the emotional baggage that weighs them down and prevents genuine connection and intimacy. Forgiveness does not mean condoning or excusing hurtful behavior but rather choosing to release the hold it has on us and move forward with compassion and understanding.

In conclusion, conflict resolution is a vital skill for fostering healthy and fulfilling relationships. By understanding the root causes of conflict, practicing active listening, validating emotions and perspectives, expressing needs and boundaries, finding common ground, collaborating on solutions, cultivating empathy and understanding, and practicing forgiveness and letting go, individuals can navigate conflict with greater sensitivity, empathy, and effectiveness. With mindfulness, empathy, and a commitment to open and honest communication, individuals can resolve conflict constructively and strengthen the bonds of their relationships, fostering greater understanding, connection, and intimacy.

Chapter 6: Integrating the Enneagram into Everyday Life

The Enneagram is not just a tool for self-awareness and personal growth—it's a comprehensive framework that can be integrated into every aspect of our lives. In this chapter, we will explore practical ways to incorporate the wisdom of the Enneagram into our everyday routines, relationships, and decision-making processes, enabling us to live more consciously, authentically, and purposefully.

Self-Reflection and Mindfulness:

One of the most powerful ways to integrate the Enneagram into everyday life is through self-reflection and mindfulness. Take time each day to reflect on your thoughts, emotions, and behaviors, and how they align with your Enneagram type. Practice mindfulness techniques such as meditation, deep breathing, or journaling to cultivate greater self-awareness and presence in the moment.

Setting Intentions and Goals:

Use the insights gained from the Enneagram to set intentions and goals that align with your core values and motivations. Identify areas for growth and development based on your Enneagram type, and create actionable steps to work towards your goals. By setting intentions rooted in self-awareness and authenticity, you can live more intentionally and purposefully each day.

Cultivating Compassion and Empathy:

The Enneagram provides valuable insights into the perspectives and experiences of others, enabling us to cultivate greater compassion and empathy in our interactions. Practice active listening, empathy, and kindness in your everyday interactions, and seek to understand the motivations and fears of those around you. By approaching others with compassion and empathy, you can foster deeper connections and create a more supportive and harmonious environment.

Navigating Relationships:

Use the Enneagram as a guide for navigating relationships with greater awareness and understanding. Recognize the Enneagram types of those closest to you, and tailor your communication and interactions accordingly. Practice patience, empathy, and compromise in your relationships, and seek to understand the underlying dynamics at play. By integrating the wisdom of the Enneagram into your relationships, you can foster deeper connection, trust, and intimacy with those you care about.

Making Decisions:

When faced with important decisions, use the insights of the Enneagram to guide your choices. Consider how each option aligns with your core values, motivations, and long-term goals, as well as the potential impact on yourself and others. Trust your intuition and inner wisdom, and listen to the guidance of your Enneagram type as you weigh your options. By making decisions from a place of self-awareness and authenticity, you can create outcomes that are in alignment with your truest self.

Managing Stress and Emotions:

The Enneagram can also be a valuable tool for managing stress and regulating emotions in everyday life. Recognize the signs of stress and emotional distress associated with your Enneagram type, and practice self-care techniques such as deep breathing, mindfulness, or physical exercise to alleviate tension and promote relaxation. Develop healthy coping strategies that honor your unique needs and preferences, and seek support from others when needed. By taking proactive steps to manage stress and emotions, you can cultivate greater resilience and well-being in your daily life.

Practicing Gratitude and Appreciation:

Incorporate gratitude and appreciation into your daily routine as a way of honoring and celebrating the unique qualities and contributions of each Enneagram type. Take time each day to express gratitude for the people, experiences, and blessings in your life, and acknowledge the strengths and gifts of yourself and others. By cultivating a mindset of gratitude and appreciation, you can foster a deeper sense of connection, abundance, and joy in your everyday life.

In conclusion, integrating the Enneagram into everyday life offers a wealth of opportunities for self-awareness, growth, and transformation. By practicing self-reflection and mindfulness, setting intentions and goals, cultivating compassion and empathy, navigating relationships, making decisions, managing stress and emotions, and practicing gratitude and appreciation, individuals can live more consciously, authentically, and purposefully each day. With dedication, intention, and a commitment to personal growth, the Enneagram can become a guiding light that illuminates our path toward greater fulfillment, connection, and well-being in all areas of our lives.

6.1 Career and Professional Development

The Enneagram isn't just a tool for personal growth—it can also be a powerful resource for navigating career and professional development. By understanding your Enneagram type and how it influences your strengths, weaknesses, motivations, and behaviors, you can make more informed decisions about your career path, enhance your professional relationships, and achieve greater success and satisfaction in the workplace. In this section, we will explore how you can leverage the insights of the Enneagram to enhance your career and professional development journey.

Understanding Your Enneagram Type in the Workplace:

Each Enneagram type brings its unique strengths and challenges to the workplace. By understanding your Enneagram type, you can gain insight into your natural talents, preferred work environments, and areas for growth. For example:

- Type 1s are detail-oriented and principled, making them well-suited for roles that require precision and adherence to standards.

- Type 2s thrive in supportive and collaborative environments, excelling in roles that involve helping and serving others.
- Type 3s are ambitious and results-driven, thriving in competitive and goal-oriented work environments.
- Type 4s are creative and introspective, often excelling in roles that allow them to express their individuality and creativity.
- Type 5s are analytical and insightful, making them valuable assets in roles that require problem-solving and strategic thinking.
- Type 6s are loyal and dependable, often excelling in roles that involve planning, organization, and risk management.
- Type 7s are innovative and adaptable, thriving in dynamic and fast-paced work environments.
- Type 8s are assertive and confident, making them natural leaders in roles that require decisiveness and authority.
- Type 9s are supportive and diplomatic, often excelling in roles that involve mediation, collaboration, and team-building.

Leveraging Your Strengths:

Once you understand your Enneagram type and its implications for your professional life, you can leverage your strengths to enhance your career success. Focus on tasks and responsibilities that align with your natural talents and interests, and seek out opportunities for growth and development in areas where you excel. By playing to your strengths, you can maximize your performance and achieve greater satisfaction and fulfillment in your career.

Addressing Your Weaknesses:

While it's essential to leverage your strengths, it's also important to address your weaknesses and areas for growth. The Enneagram can help you identify areas where you may struggle or encounter challenges in the workplace and develop strategies for improvement. Seek feedback from colleagues, mentors, or supervisors, and be open to constructive criticism and opportunities for growth. By acknowledging and addressing your weaknesses, you can become a more well-rounded and effective professional.

Enhancing Professional Relationships:

The Enneagram can also be a valuable tool for enhancing your professional relationships and communication skills. By understanding the Enneagram types of your colleagues, supervisors, and clients, you can adapt your communication style and approach to better meet their needs and preferences. Practice active listening, empathy, and collaboration in your interactions, and seek to understand the perspectives and motivations of others. By fostering positive and productive relationships in the workplace, you can enhance teamwork, morale, and overall performance.

Setting Career Goals and Objectives:

Use the insights of the Enneagram to inform your career goals and objectives. Consider how your Enneagram type influences your long-term aspirations, values, and priorities, and set goals that align with your authentic self. Focus on goals that resonate with your core values and motivations, and develop a plan for achieving them. By setting clear and meaningful career goals, you can stay motivated and focused on your professional development journey.

Navigating Career Transitions:

The Enneagram can also be a valuable resource for navigating career transitions and changes. Whether you're considering a new job opportunity, seeking a promotion, or transitioning to a new industry, the Enneagram can provide insights into your preferences, strengths, and areas for growth. Take time to reflect on your career goals and aspirations, and consider how different opportunities align with your Enneagram type. By making informed decisions based on self-awareness and authenticity, you can navigate career transitions with confidence and clarity.

Cultivating Work-Life Balance:

Finally, use the insights of the Enneagram to cultivate a healthy work-life balance that honors your needs and priorities outside of work. Recognize the importance of self-care, relaxation, and leisure activities in maintaining your well-being and overall satisfaction with life. Set boundaries around your work commitments and prioritize activities that nourish your mind, body, and spirit. By cultivating a balanced approach to work and life, you can avoid burnout and maintain long-term career success and fulfillment.

In conclusion, the Enneagram offers valuable insights and strategies for enhancing your career and professional development journey. By understanding your Enneagram type and its implications for your strengths, weaknesses, motivations, and behaviors, you can make more informed decisions about your career path, leverage your strengths, address your weaknesses, enhance professional relationships, set meaningful goals.

6.2 Health and Wellness: Integrating Enneagram Insights for Well-Being

Our physical and mental well-being is fundamental to living a fulfilling and meaningful life. The Enneagram, with its deep insights into personality and behavior, can be a powerful tool for enhancing our health and wellness practices. In this section, we will explore how we can integrate Enneagram insights into our approach to health and wellness, enabling us to cultivate greater self-awareness, balance, and vitality in our lives.

Understanding Enneagram Types and Health Patterns:

Each Enneagram type has its unique patterns of behavior, coping mechanisms, and stress responses that can impact our physical and mental health. By understanding these patterns, we can gain insight into how our Enneagram type influences our health and wellness practices. For example:

- Type 1s may be prone to perfectionism and self-criticism, leading to stress-related health issues such as tension headaches or digestive problems.

- Type 2s may struggle with boundary-setting and self-care, potentially leading to burnout or exhaustion from overextending themselves to help others.
- Type 3s may prioritize achievement and success at the expense of their health, leading to stress-related conditions such as anxiety or high blood pressure.
- Type 4s may be susceptible to mood disorders or emotional eating patterns when they feel misunderstood or disconnected from others.
- Type 5s may neglect their physical health in favor of intellectual pursuits, potentially leading to issues such as poor posture or lack of exercise.
- Type 6s may experience anxiety or hypervigilance, leading to chronic stress-related conditions such as insomnia or digestive problems.
- Type 7s may struggle with impulsivity or addictive behaviors, potentially leading to issues such as overeating or substance abuse.
- Type 8s may experience anger-related health issues such as high blood pressure or muscle tension when they feel threatened or out of control.
- Type 9s may suppress their emotions or avoid conflict, potentially leading to issues such as emotional eating or disordered eating patterns.

Cultivating Self-Awareness and Mindfulness:

Self-awareness is key to making informed choices about our health and wellness. By understanding our Enneagram type and its impact on our thoughts, emotions, and behaviors, we can cultivate greater self-awareness and mindfulness in our daily lives. Practice observing your thoughts, feelings, and physical sensations without judgment, and notice how they may be influenced by your Enneagram type. By cultivating mindfulness, we can become more attuned to our body's signals and make healthier choices that support our well-being.

Tailoring Wellness Practices to Your Enneagram Type:

Just as each Enneagram type has its unique patterns of behavior, it also has distinct wellness needs and preferences. Tailoring your wellness practices to your Enneagram type can help you create a more personalized and effective approach to health and well-being. For example:

- Type 1s may benefit from structured wellness practices such as yoga or meditation to cultivate mindfulness and reduce perfectionistic tendencies.
- Type 2s may benefit from self-compassion practices and boundary-setting exercises to prioritize their own needs and avoid burnout.
- Type 3s may benefit from stress-management techniques such as deep breathing or progressive muscle relaxation to alleviate tension and promote relaxation.
- Type 4s may benefit from expressive arts therapies such as journaling or creative writing to explore their emotions and foster self-expression.
- Type 5s may benefit from regular exercise routines or outdoor activities to stay physically active and connected to their bodies.
- Type 6s may benefit from grounding techniques such as mindfulness or meditation to alleviate anxiety and promote a sense of calm.

- Type 7s may benefit from mindfulness practices such as mindful eating or mindful walking to cultivate presence and reduce impulsivity.
- Type 8s may benefit from practices that promote emotional release and stress relief such as martial arts or boxing to channel their energy constructively.
- Type 9s may benefit from practices that promote self-awareness and assertiveness such as assertiveness training or conflict resolution skills to express their needs and desires more effectively.

Building Healthy Habits and Routines:

Consistency is key to maintaining optimal health and wellness. By building healthy habits and routines that align with your Enneagram type, you can create a sustainable foundation for well-being. Identify specific wellness goals that resonate with your Enneagram type, and develop a plan for incorporating them into your daily life. Whether it's setting aside time for exercise, practicing mindfulness, or prioritizing self-care activities, find routines that support your physical, mental, and emotional health.

Nurturing Supportive Relationships:

Social support is essential for maintaining health and well-being, and our Enneagram type can influence the types of relationships we seek out and how we interact with others. Cultivate relationships that nourish and support your well-being, and seek out individuals who understand and appreciate your Enneagram type. Surround yourself with people who uplift and inspire you, and avoid toxic or draining relationships that undermine your health and happiness.

Seeking Professional Support:

While self-awareness and self-care practices are essential components of health and wellness, it's also important to seek professional support when needed. If you're struggling with chronic health issues, mental health concerns, or stress-related symptoms, don't hesitate to reach out to a qualified healthcare provider or mental health professional for guidance and support. They can provide personalized recommendations and interventions tailored to your individual needs and circumstances.

In conclusion, integrating Enneagram insights into our approach to health and wellness can enhance our self-awareness, balance, and vitality in profound ways. By understanding how our Enneagram type influences our health patterns, cultivating self-awareness and mindfulness, tailoring wellness practices to our Enneagram type, building healthy habits and routines, nurturing supportive relationships, and seeking professional support when needed, we can create a holistic approach to health and well-being that honors our unique needs and preferences. With dedication, intention, and a commitment to self-care, we can cultivate greater health, happiness, and resilience in our lives, empowering us to thrive in body, mind, and spirit.

6.3 Spiritual Growth and Mindfulness: Embracing the Enneagram Path

Spiritual growth and mindfulness are integral aspects of the human experience, offering pathways to greater meaning, connection, and fulfillment in life. The Enneagram, with its profound insights into personality and behavior, can be a transformative tool for deepening our spiritual journey and cultivating mindfulness in our everyday lives. In this section, we will explore how we can embrace the Enneagram path to enhance our spiritual growth and mindfulness practices.

Understanding the Spiritual Dimensions of the Enneagram:

At its core, the Enneagram is not just a personality typing system—it's a profound spiritual map that invites us to explore the depths of our souls and awaken to our true nature. Each Enneagram type reflects a unique expression of divine essence, as well as the obstacles and illusions that obscure our connection to our higher selves. By understanding our Enneagram type and its underlying spiritual themes, we can embark on a journey of self-discovery and transformation that leads us closer to the divine within.

Cultivating Self-Awareness and Presence:

Self-awareness is the foundation of spiritual growth and mindfulness. By cultivating self-awareness through the lens of the Enneagram, we can become more attuned to our thoughts, emotions, and behaviors, and develop greater clarity and insight into our innermost selves. Practice mindfulness techniques such as meditation, breathwork, or body scanning to cultivate presence and awareness in the present moment. Notice how your Enneagram type influences your thoughts and behaviors, and observe them with compassionate curiosity and non-judgment.

Embracing the Virtues of Your Enneagram Type:

Each Enneagram type embodies a unique set of virtues—qualities that reflect our highest potential and deepest aspirations. By embracing the virtues of your Enneagram type, you can align with your truest self and embody qualities such as love, courage, wisdom, and compassion. Reflect on the virtues associated with your Enneagram type, and strive to cultivate them in your thoughts, words, and actions. Practice acts of kindness, generosity, and forgiveness that reflect the divine within you, and embody the virtues that lead to greater spiritual growth and fulfillment.

Transforming Limiting Beliefs and Patterns:

The Enneagram reveals the unconscious beliefs and patterns that shape our lives and limit our potential for growth and fulfillment. By shining a light on these patterns, we can begin to unravel the illusions that keep us stuck in suffering and separation from our true essence. Explore the core fears and desires of your Enneagram type, and inquire into the beliefs and behaviors that arise from them. Practice self-inquiry and reflection to challenge and transcend these limiting beliefs, and cultivate new ways of thinking and being that align with your highest truth.

Navigating Spiritual Challenges and Growth Opportunities:

The spiritual journey is not always smooth sailing—it often involves facing challenges and obstacles that test our faith and resilience. The Enneagram can help us navigate these challenges with greater wisdom and grace, providing insights into the spiritual lessons and growth opportunities they offer. When faced with difficulties, reflect on the spiritual themes and patterns at play in your life, and consider how they invite you to deepen your understanding and connection to the divine. Embrace challenges as opportunities for growth and transformation, and trust in the wisdom of your Enneagram type to guide you on your journey.

Cultivating Compassion and Connection:

Compassion is the heart of spiritual growth and mindfulness. By cultivating compassion for ourselves and others, we can dissolve the barriers that separate us and awaken to the interconnectedness of all life. Practice loving-kindness meditation or compassion practices to cultivate empathy and kindness towards yourself and others. Recognize the inherent worth and dignity of every being, and treat yourself and others with kindness, respect, and understanding. By embodying compassion in our thoughts, words, and actions, we can create a more compassionate and connected world.

Engaging in Sacred Practices and Rituals:

Sacred practices and rituals can deepen our spiritual connection and create sacred space for reflection, prayer, and contemplation. Explore spiritual practices that resonate with your Enneagram type, such as meditation, prayer, yoga, or sacred chanting. Create rituals that honor your spiritual path and invite you to connect with the divine within. Whether it's lighting a candle, setting an intention, or engaging in a daily gratitude practice, find practices that nourish your soul and deepen your connection to the divine.

In conclusion, the Enneagram offers profound insights and guidance for enhancing our spiritual growth and mindfulness practices. By understanding the spiritual dimensions of the Enneagram, cultivating self-awareness and presence, embracing the virtues of our Enneagram type, transforming limiting beliefs and patterns, navigating spiritual challenges and growth opportunities, cultivating compassion and connection, and engaging in sacred practices and rituals, we can embark on a journey of self-discovery and transformation that leads us closer to the divine within. With dedication, intention, and a commitment to spiritual growth, we can awaken to our true nature and live more consciously, authentically, and joyfully in alignment with our highest truth.

Conclusion:

In "The Enneagram: A Comprehensive Guide to Understanding Personality Types and Unlocking the Secrets of the Enneagram to Discover Your True Self and Improve Relationships," we have embarked on a journey of self-discovery and transformation, guided by the profound wisdom of the Enneagram.

Throughout this comprehensive guide, we have explored the nine Enneagram personality types, delving deep into their core motivations, fears, desires, and patterns of behavior. We have gained insight into how our Enneagram type influences every aspect of our lives, from our career choices and relationships to our health and spiritual growth.

But the Enneagram is more than just a tool for understanding ourselves—it's a map for navigating the complexities of human nature and fostering greater compassion, empathy, and connection in our relationships. By understanding the Enneagram types of those around us, we can cultivate deeper understanding and acceptance, bridging the gap between our differences and fostering greater harmony and cooperation.

As we conclude our journey with the Enneagram, remember that self-awareness is the key to unlocking the secrets of the Enneagram and discovering your true self. Embrace the journey of self-discovery with curiosity, compassion, and courage, knowing that each step brings you closer to the essence of who you are and the infinite possibilities that await you.

May this guide serve as a beacon of light on your Enneagram journey, illuminating the path to greater self-awareness, personal growth, and transformation. May you embrace the wisdom of the Enneagram with an open heart and mind, knowing that the journey to self-discovery is a lifelong adventure filled with wonder, insight, and possibility.

Thank you for joining me on this transformative journey with the Enneagram. May you continue to explore, evolve, and thrive as you unlock the secrets of your true self and cultivate deeper connections with those around you. Remember, the Enneagram is not just a tool—it's a roadmap to living a more authentic, meaningful, and fulfilling life.